BREAK

Mikael Josephsen

Translated from the Danish by Nina Sokol

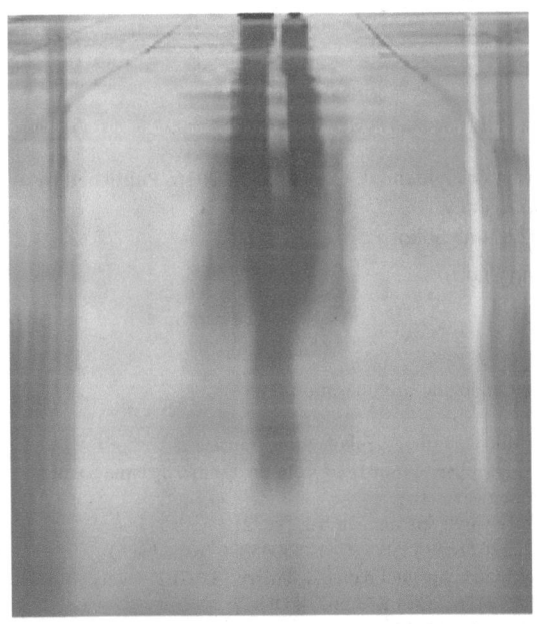

Spuyten Duyvil
New York City

Special thanks to The Danish Arts Foundation for financial
support towards the translation and publication of this book.

Danish Arts
Foundation

ISBN 978-1-956005-89-9

Library of Congress Cataloging-in-Publication Data

Names: Josephsen, Mikael, author. | Sokol, Nina, translator.
Title: Break / Mikael Josephsen ; translated from the Danish by Nina Sokol.
Other titles: Knæk. English
Description: New York City : Spuyten Duyvil, [2022]
Identifiers: LCCN 2022027648 | ISBN 9781956005899 (paperback)
Subjects: LCSH: Psychiatric hospital patients--Poetry. | LCGFT: Poetry.
Classification: LCC PT8176.2.O84 K53 2022 | DDC
  839.811/74--dc23/eng/20220613
LC record available at https://lccn.loc.gov/2022027648

"And I know their road
From having walked it
More than a hundred times already
A hundred times more than halfway
Less elderly or more bruised
They're going to reach its end
They walk in silence
The hopeless"

Jacques Brel "The Hopeless"

"La la la la la la
la la la la la
la la la la la
la la la la la..."

Ulf Lundell

SVENDBORG, CHRISTMAS, 2014, PSYCHIATRIC WARD, P3.

I'm thinking about how you are doing
no, I'm thinking about how I am doing
without you.
I am fine, thanks.
The nurses are generous with the needle
and I have been given a pair of long
underwear
winter has, after all, arrived and it is cold in the smoker's room
where I am building a gallows out of cigarette stubs
from which you will hang
which I naturally won't tell the chief of staff
or I'll be put into the straitjacket,
and risk getting electrical currents shot through my body
and salivating in the cookies
which may be messages from intelligent forms of life on other planets
if I must say something
then it is
that the days are
at
least
passing.

*

It smells of hash in the ward today
the psychotics are smoking

other than that it is peaceful here

Astrid got electrical currents shot through her body
yesterday so her screams no longer fill the halls
Lonni is on duty
along with Sussi so some Benzos might
fall off along the
way.

I lie in bed ringing the bell
as if I was in a hotel.

Yesterday Solveig jabbed her hand with a fork
usually she eats using plastic ware
but she stole it
from the chief physician's office.

My blood tests are still fucked
cancer cancer cancer
always cancer
and the constant paralysis in my arm
I miss writing.

The lady now comes to place electrodes
on my feet and chest
those are the jewels of the mental patient.

There is juice in the plastic cup on the night table.

I have lice and my son
has come to shave off my hair

I stand, bald, in hospital clothes
but am wearing a plastic bracelet that has my
CRS number on it
They have taken my telephone

My son leaves shortly after
I have been given the injection.

I turn inwards,
lying in a foetal position,
denying my own birth.

My sister is in Ward 1
She has gotten electrical currents shot through her
because she set fire to the ward
we are not allowed to visit one another

the cartoon characters are after her
they step out of the magazine

I myself am practically normal
I may have a little problem with the bottle
but I can recite my name when
the blood test lady asks me to.

Our childhood is what caused it all
Glen has been transported to the violent ward
he attacked one of Ulla's visitors.

I am now going to take an after-dinner nap
that is the best thing about being here
the clean white bed sheets
against the dirty dreams.

Someone is walking up and
down the hallway
I toss and turn
switch on the light

Someone else is coughing next door
there is the creak of a bed
I drink to calm
my nervous system

I drink so that the sounds
won't be sharp razor blades
I drink to make your face disappear
no, to make everything disappear

But tonight I miss you like
ears stuffed with cotton wool

I try to masturbate
force my thoughts
Hell, I'm just trying to survive
the patient
stops by my door
wanders on

Outside a red light bleeds the darkness up
I imagine a wrist
an open pulse

I ring the bell again and say
that there are rats at the foot of the bed, their teeth are orange
from the infection

Again, a thermometer up the ass
a doctor comes and shines a light into my eyes,
the flashlight is as small as a ballpoint pen
dilated pupils
200 milligrams phenobarbital, she says

I immediately pull my underpants down and
turn my ass out to the room
irritated over how much time it takes to
draw fluid from the needle.

Finally a finger that chafes the cheek, the shot
that tightens and loosens, it is like sobbing
after a long-term wound, it is like finding God
in emptiness.

Like when the police picked up my father
and locked him away.

I can't get it out of my head
that there are small receptacles filled
with alcohol hanging in the bathrooms
that she has left me
I don't know anybody
you don't know anybody here
the schizophrenics receive visits
that's the way it is
and we sit with our plastic forks and eat
in a room
that sometimes disappears
one of the young girls has grown a moustache
and her voice has grown dark because of the medicine
just like my grandmother
on the walls there are pictures painted by former madmen
the one above the sink depicts
a preposterous eye
purple
I guzzle an egg sandwich
orange
the door is locked
there is a fence around the building
a plane in the sky
if you bend over a little and turn your head to the side
you can see a trolley with thermo jugs
and plastic cups
today they're serving herring

A lady is walking up and
down the hall
she is consoling a doll
I'm considering stealing it
from her

I walk over to the coffee table
those are poisonous Søren says
pointing at the milk carton

Gert comes dragging his feet
there are microphones in the scripts
when you skim them, perhaps a priest
or continue walking,
he says.

Ulla drops the cheese cutter
and bends down to get it
Uffe kicks it further away

then she takes a plastic knife
and slashes it through the air
at him

I could lie with that doll and play that it was
my wife
who is the one with the doll
I ask
I have no home here
with things
things are an extension of the skin
she's just a nut
Gert says.

I drink my coffee and walk over to the cage
the lady with the doll bothers me
I say to the guard on duty

Bothers you how?
I can't stand hearing that goddamn kid's screams

She must be moved, the doll must be burned
my head is exploding.

I will not take a bath before I get an injection
if you get more injections your heart will stop beating
then make it stop beating
get into the bath, you don't smell good
it's the cancer
you don't have cancer
then look at my blood tests and the blood in my urine
it all looks much better than yesterday, let's get you into the bath
if I get an injection
we'll see about that after you've taken a bath
look at my toe, do you think it's cancer?
No, you hit it by accident
it's all blue
that's what happens
but the bruise has been there long
I'm putting some clean clothes here and there are towels in the bathroom
and I'll be getting an injection then
we'll see
you just promised an injection if I took a bath
no I didn't
yes, you did, I'm going to make a complaint you can't make a promise and then
not keep it I have cancer
You don't have cancer
Then look at the tests, then look at the tests
I think you'll feel better after a bath
I think I'll feel better after an injection.

I piss in the urinal
in the window to the world
and I apologize a little
for the size

You should have seen it when I was young
I say to the young student nurse
Now you're boasting

I miss the mark

let's hope there's no blood or sugar in it today
she takes the urinal in her rubber-gloved
hand and leaves

I stand in wet pants remembering
the whips of wet towels
the girls giggling
but

with Frandsen it's even worse
it's whispered that he likes children
and sliced it off
he doesn't even come out for meals

I want to do it personally
Hanne says

I feel for mine in my pants
it's still there

imagine
screwing the student nurse
feel something
do something else besides
standing in wet pants
satisfied with not being
Frandsen.

As a boy my cups would stand on the shelf
like my father's

Here I have a bottle of urine standing there

I think of it every time
I pass the table tennis table
the two bats, the net and
the ball no one can find

I always fondle the green,
smooth, surface with my finger,
straighten the net

walk to the podium in my club t-shirt,
shorts,
the spectator's standing ovation

my father at the finish line, following in the footsteps of death,
past the turn off at Tuborg, up toward the judge's stand
while the horse foams at the bridle
I should have been a winner
second best is the biggest loser

the only thing I'm really good at is
bewailing my way to the next injection

I can shiver and sweat, have a fever
I don't want to wean off it
I will go on to the bitter end
in this strong field of losers.

I woke up from an excavator
standing in the ward
my hands were smeared with blood

later on Lonni said that was silly
as she kept a straight face, shut
her eyes across time

just as my grandmother used to do
when the doctor had
given her an injection

I cannot say for sure what it is like
I am not entirely myself
It's as though I've been torn
down

as the dosage of medicine continually goes up
It won't be long before the first snowdrop
shows up by the hospital wall
is what Lonni says
who has been keeping an eye on it

I don't have the words for it all today
I can't say it
it is gone.

Father
you have no idea how much you scare me
I'm so afraid you might die
I can't sleep at night anymore
mother can't sleep either
won't you please stop
drinking when you are released
I won't come and get more schnapps anymore
I won't come at all
I don't have a father
you won't have a son if you do it
do you prefer the bottle to me.

It is just that
I say to the nurse
my eyes like knives
my tongue like a lash,
if I don't get that needle right now
I'll kick the medicine cabinet
and what do you think will happen then
her smile is a winner's
and I know
I have lost
everything
I am no one here
diagnosed as psychotic,
bipolar
and wouldn't mind seeing
this hospital go up in flames
I go back to the ward
crawl into bed
choke the pillow like a teddy-bear
it is two hours before the next injection
I go out to the bathroom and tear down
the alcohol dispenser
and drink and
go into the next toilet,
not until the third
do I meet two nurses
Bjørn and Otto
What do you think you're doing
they say
It's because they won't give me an injection

I say, throwing up on Bjørn
Otto gets a splash on his shoe
You're damn well not drinking
what we disinfect our hands in?
Are you mad?
Then get the injection,
get it, damn it.

WARD: *PSY P3 UNIT (SVENDBORG)*
HOSPITAL: PSYCHIATRIC SERVICES REGION SOUTHERN DENMARK

*Up at around 1 am, asking where he is, whether the juice is standing
on the shelf in his room and other delirious questions. He also thinks
he has been on a camping trip.*

You were on a real trip there
Lonni says as she velcroes my arm
until it starts throbbing

Sweden Sweden Sweden
my paradise in the woods
I had forgotten
Oh, life.

I turn my ass to her and receive the thermometer
It cuts me off for a moment
but I take it like a whore

Green woods flicker before my eyes
a dive in the lake
Helga Johansson in the shade with snuff
you were all dazed,
claiming you were going to a concert
with Ulf Lundel
as though that's a name everyone should know

It is God I say when the thermometer
is pulled out
the pain again but

One line remains stuck:
If this is winter spring must be on its way
If this is winter spring must be
on its way.

Everyone is tip-toeing
through the ward this morning,
there are faint whispers

last night I dreamed
that I spurted on a child
in a street
in an alley
in Nazi Denmark

It wasn't my dream
but it was dreamed in my mind
and they know it

Everyone knows it
the train that ticks past
the night table's wheels across the linoleum
and the bed clothes

that deep down I am a pedophile like Frandsen
and even though I open my mouth
and try to say
that it is the new medicine
no words co-
me out.

I now know what will happen
for the rest of my life
I'm preparing myself
developing eyes in the back of my head

photographs of me everywhere
in the ward
which is a city
of addicts.

I have been given permission to
go to the kiosk with Lonni today

We take the elevator down
together with an orderly and an empty bed
I'm going to get a Coca Cola Light and pack of Cecil

Lonni says she's googled me
and told the other nurses
who I am
and some of them have bought my books
and some are sorry
that they didn't know
because it would have been different then,
she says.

There are many customers at the kiosk
and while Lonni is talking with another nurse
I grab a bottle of wine
put it in my pants

Hold on there,
what do you think you're doing
the kiosk lady has caught sight of me
and I must return the wine
but they don't call the police

He's an author, Lonni says
which makes it more understandable

It can't be easy to always have to think up things
as the elevator goes back up
and I step into the ward like
a star.

Father
I'm not visiting you
because you acted that way at my confirmation
and now you only call when you want me to get you some schnapps
I hope you have a merry Christmas
I'm living with a good friend,
you know, the girl who stopped smoking pot.

*

I imagine that you're decorating the place for Christmas now
did you also put fairy lights
on the little tree
by the gable
how time flies
I'm not angry anymore by the way
the new medicine mixes well with the old one
even though I am tired
but no longer young anymore
the doctor says
I was wondering whether I could get some money from the house
I owe someone here a little cash
his eyes look pretty sick
it is not easy here
the whole thing
but it will work out
tonight there are hymns
with piano accompaniment
it is also important to remember the good things
do you think you could
get me a gun
I hope there are no mice
in the house
I know how you hate mice.

Patient 1: We have the same surname.

Patient 2: Yes, it's strange.

P1: Perhaps they've switched our medicine.

P2: What makes you think that

P1: There could be many reasons

P2: I'm sure they have it under control

P1: Exactly, they know what they're doing.

P2: I just don't see why

P1: Yes, well, there you are, they know what they're doing

P2: I see what you mean

P1: Yes, it's cunning, but if we switch medicines, then they're back where they started

P2: Unless they've already taken that into consideration

P1: It would be like them to be that cunning

P2: Then there's nothing we can do

P1: You see what I mean, then.

P2: Yes, we are trapped

P1: It's gotten colder

P3: Do you have a light

P1: I never lend my lighter to anyone.

P2: Here you go.

P3: thank you.

P1 they can make microphones and cameras so small that they can put them in the pills.

P2 so small

P1 Can't you see it? Can't you see why they switched them?

P2: you may be on to something

P1 no, they're the ones who are on to something, now they can see us from inside and by switching our medicine, they can hide behind it.

P2: It's a downright disgrace

P3: It's gotten colder

P2 Yes

P1 Are you one of them

P3: One of who?

P1: you see? We don't stand a chance.

Jesus lives

Last night I dreamed
or was it yesterday afternoon
about us and the house
I had moved back in
and the kids had been wound
back in time
and the apple tree was blooming
but suddenly I was in my childhood home
and all the people became
distorted
their faces looked like
rubber gloves
there was room after room
and every time you opened the door to
a new one you would get hit by an
ever potent stench of horse
I don't really know why I'm telling you this
I also opened a drawer
overflowing with mites
Today we are going to go out for a walk
The blood test came in this morning
everything looks good
I was allowed to visit my sister yesterday
she was lying on her back looking up at the ceiling
and drooling a little
but she's no longer sick
everything tastes like horse today
I know I broke into the neighbor's
and the farm
and threatened your life
but I am, after all, only
human.

Jesus lives

he's just not here at the moment.

There should be all kinds of
moments
Ulla says as she pulls down her pants

there are no nurses
and she thrusts her abdomen forth
and wriggles a little

her cunt is brown
I prefer them to be black
turn back toward the TV set
the birth mark

I keep thinking over and over that's it's grown
malignant melanoma
the frightening word keeps whirling about
in my mind
slashes into it like a snake

I will have another doctor look at it
no doctor
is to look at it
it stretches from my shoulder across my chest
it looks the face of C.V Jørgensen

Put your pants back on
You can't stand here in the common room
looking like that
my cunt is bored
My CUNT is bored
MY CUNT IS BORED

Then the thriller series begins
I've already lost track of the plot
after the first scene

malignant melanoma is the suspect
crimes keep taking place on the body
the scene of the crime

There should be all kinds of moments
Ulla pulls up her pants.

Rags have been brought up
from the cellar

It's wonderful to be working again
while listening to the radio
as your thoughts follow the rags
and your hands lack nothing

and juice and cookies are served

a morning like this at the ward
is something everyone
should have the opportunity to experience.

You always hear about the bad things
but reality is much more nuanced
says Lonni
and Glenn looks up
from his rag
smiling with his black mouth

and a tiny streak of light seeps through the crack in the curtains
as the head physician passes us
and nods

Today is a day where things are going better
that is so clear
it is easy to dip the cookie
into the juice
and swallow

Someone in the second ward
threatened a nurse yesterday
saying he would slit

her throat
and her children's

I would never go that far

especially not now where there is talk of
allowing me to go home with an attendant
and water my flowers
and check my mail
the head physician nodded

But now I'm not sure I'd dare
someone may see me
I would exist in the building
again
and I remember nothing about the days
up to the ambulance

I'm thinking I may have raped
someone or strangled a child
who just hasn't been found in the garage yet

or I may have committed masked robbery at Shop Rite
this idea of a day out won't do
I say to Lonni
I can't with the pains I have in my foot
I wouldn't make it up the stairs

the flowers I have are made of plastic

His face is blue
with yellow eyes
and looks like a beach ball

and now he's the one whimpering
and begging for injections
when he gets up every so often
I say it will get better

but that's just to console him
everyone knows it will all get much worse

soon he will be able to see
without there being a cobweb between his eyes,
be able to feel without his nerves going into cramps
and he will realize that the nightmare
is progressing

and the only way around it is a new booze binge
a new admission to the hospital

but for now we'll let him lie there
as his blood tests are examined under a magnifying glass
his urine dissected
and the world
that big animal
stands agape
for now we'll let him lie there.

I'm in the bathroom masturbating
I want it to keep working
despite the medicine
maybe it has cancer
in which case I know what is done
cut
cut Mr. Cockless
so you ended up becoming that sissy your father loathed after all
a woman forced to suck
anal
once we found a porn magazine
that had pictures of a cunt
close-ups
it was ugly as hell
but I thought about it at school during classes
and was allowed to do an assignment
called the cunt
and faggot Olsen thought it was good
Faggot Olsen was the only one who ever said anything
nice to me as a child
I remain limp
try again
I remain limp
someone knocks on the door
yeah, yeah
I know what they do
with people like me

It's a little before lunch,
masked terrorists enter
the ward

they shoot down everyone and everything

the ward is now filled with corpses
holes in the walls

I tell the press that I survived
by playing dead

it comes on the news
right before dinner

there are still police everywhere
and I shake as I reach
for the coffee

My grandmother
thought that my toy rifle
was meant to shoot her
so she was taken
away for several months

she came back home and
sat silently in the sofa,
pushing her dentures
to the front of her mouth

I loved my grandmother

Other than that it's quiet today
I'm just lying here in the ward
waiting for a life
with the dead
I follow a speck of dust as it sinks and rises
sinks and rises.

In a way I'm not lying here
it is not me
just the shell
and the memory of my grandmother
I can't imagine a future
without my BEING grandmother

My grandfather was a cold monkey

The last thing I heard at my father's funeral
was that he had been beaten with a board
in the basement
and been carried up as a bloody bundle
my grandfather always hummed
while grinding his teeth

my aunt died from drug abuse
otherwise everyone is mentally ill on both sides
of the family
not that it means anything
but you end up thinking about those things
when lying in bed

My sister screamed as the hearse drove from the church
with my mother lying in the coffin.
It is Tuesday.

There's a new
patient today
he has tattoos on his face

I am scared
I ask to be moved
I don't dare leave
the ground floor

he is as bald as an egg
and his scalp is tattooed as well
on the back of his neck a black inked-ox is split
the skull that blossoms in red

He's sitting in the middle of the sofa
in the day room
both his arms are resting on the back of a pillow
he is smoking even though
it's forbidden

they say that he sleeps
with a gun under his mattress
he's managed the whole hash scene in Odense
and killed immigrants
like flies

Lonni takes me by the hand

he's siting there in the day room and sobbing
with his head in his hands
as snot runs down his chin
and two nurses sit with a comforting hand on him each

I'm just trying to do my best
he sniffles
and I continue to hum
behind Lonni's back.

It has been carefully planned
Lonni wants to kill me

She has been planning it for a long time
in collaboration with my ex-wife and kids
I heard them clearly whispering
the police have been notified

God has spoken from
the highest place above

I will perish from the poison
they put in my coffee
and no longer be a burden
I will be carried off like a corpse
my soul will go to hell
that is what we are here practicing for.

A plastic Paki has just entered
he goes around mimicking
that he's slitting someone's neck and
says we will all burn in hell
in the name of Allah.

He walks around with the Koran tucked under his arm
it doesn't matter which book
and he has a long beard
sometimes he let's it all go
and is just peaceful Joe from
Ishøj.

Then he eats pork and laughs
but the next second he is Mohammad once again
spitting out fiery words

he also has a third state of being
right after taking his medicine
in which he drools and dozes
while growling like a bear

we are all sitting in front of the television
hoping it will be John who wakes up this time.

I hear them talking behind the door
saying that I'm a pig
because I shit my bed
at night

But it slowly runs its course.

I break into a run
down the hallway
I go through the door like a ghost
to where my sister is

I find her in the common room

I clasp her to my bosom
and sob.

I come walking carrying a turd in my hands
knock on the door of the glass cage

the office on duty's lipstick
when she sees it

It's sick, I say
I would like the doctor to take a look at it
You can't just stand there
with that in your hands

She accompanies me back to the common room
we put the turd in a bag
she has promised to deliver it for analysis

the word analysis makes me lie down
like I lay on the examination couch
for fifteen years

The psychologist would say something along the lines of:
that is your language right now
you are speaking in symbols

It may very well be that he is right
but that turd has got to be
examined now

It has to be dissected and examined for blood,
checked thoroughly,
it has to be taken seriously.

Now Lonni
comes in
wearing white pantyhose
and thigh-highs
nothing else
No, she is wearing a dress
high heels
is there anything I can do
she says and sits
on the edge of the bed
suck my dick I say throwing
the blanket aside
If that is what the Lord says
If that is the Lord's wish
Shut up
or I'll put out my cigarette on
your fat mealy thighs
taking you firmly
Now
Lonni comes in
wearing her
nurse's uniform
is there anything I
can do she says

sitting on the edge of the bed
sitting on the edge fo the bed
sitting on the edge fo the bed

I would like a glass of juice.

*

As though I don't already
that he fucks better than I do
gentle and hard
the way you like it
and he probably doesn't read your diary
he earns good money
and doesn't write books about your life together
perhaps I should get
surgical shoes
I've been notified by the police
that I am not to contact you
tomorrow a new tree will be put in the smoker's room
plastic
but it will look nice
I'll probably be let out soon
and I won't be allowed to approach the house within a 500 meter radius
even though it's actually still my house
but don't worry
I won't kill you
and I won't harm the new one
it's stopped snowing
in contrast, the rain is still hitting the window pane
there is still lice in the ward

I have to have a nurse come with me to the bathroom
she has to see my turd
it is black
I say
It is brown
she says
black
brown
black brown
I flush
as the proof
leaks out in the sewage system
to be dissected by rats and
wind through the sewage pipes
below
the city
with its hospital
and patients
fighting over dark colors
in each his own white cell.

There is television in the ward tonight
when I close my eyes
I see violent porn
it always comes after the night medicine.

I feel like strangling my kids

And I can't feel the left
side of my cheek
the words crumble and the ward is like being
in a rubber boat.

I don't know much
about the other patients.
Søren with the gloves is very scared of bacteria
and other of God
he's constantly ducking and looking up

Another is God
and looks down

there are cookies to go with the coffee
and every now and then an arm reaches out
to draw one in like
prey.

On TV they are dancing in fancy clothes
and cheerful but stern judges
judge

the cookies have been mixed and the ones with chocolate
are gone

the rain is tapping on the window
and I wonder why the tongue always
looks for the sharpest tooth in the mouth.

So many diagnoses
I've never seen anything like it
it's almost like a bouquet

But, of course, it's in the course of an entire life

Alcoholic with a personality disorder
hash addict
pill addict
bipolar
borderline psychotic
pseudo psychopath
anxiety disorder
PTSD

Actually I'm just afraid of dying
of cancer like my
mom

The head physician turns his wedding ring
then he starts tapping the table top
rhythmically

no, it's impressive

I look out the window, another hospital building
I merge into it
am a stone
a window pane looking in
at myself

I can't
even fit the large sizes

that's how it is for most people here
last night I dreamed I was a fast and nasty rat

Now I'm not a psychologist
but it could have to do with the sewage
pipes underneath the city

they have started to drill upwards and listen

there are microphones pretty much everywhere
and you are filmed
at night

in your mind

they use it all in courtrooms and send
it on live TV
that you are guilty.

Couldn't
do
anything
but
stand
under
porch-
roofs
lie
curled
up
like
cigarette
packs
on
hard
benches
sign
in
the
apartment
block
and
started
on
the
ambulances
again
I
crossed
all
boundaries
I
crossed

everyone's
boundaries
it
isn't
possible
to
keep
the
ocean
at
bay
by
giving
the
finger
you
can't
love
yourself
then
someone
else
will
be
missing
no
one
can
bear
seeing
thier
mother
die
of

cancer
though
that's
no
excuse
it's
just
a
chain
I
want
you
to
know
that
you
can
always
go
further
down
than
down
there
is
room
under
under
a
double
mother
well
that's
where

I
lived
I
live
in
the
apartment
block
you
can
be
medicated
for
TV
and
the
streets
where
the
pharmacies
light
up
like
lit
ships
sure
we
were
dysfunctional
I
love
the
liqour
it

is
a
break
from
oneself
in
the
apartment
block
I
hung
up
pictures
until
I
got
a
home
I
fried
food
and
figured
out
how
to
work
the
washing
machine
in
the
basement
but

being
bored
is
what
one
misses
and
then
that
damned
fear
of
the
Greenlander
from
tomorrow
til
tomorrow
rats
in
the
bed
rats
everywhere
the
body
is
a miniature
of
childhood
for
us
hypochondriacs
you

could
have
been
here
to
help
me
with
the
duvet
cover
I
have
crawled
down
under
it
this
is not
literature
I'm
through
with
the
fancy
stuff
I
only
write
for
you
you
put
me

on
an
ice
floe
I
now
emerge
from
the
fog
am
the
fog
anyway
but
we
watch
terror
on
TV
I
dare
to
stand
by
my
pain
how
badly
I
feel
my
private
terror

I
mow
down
myself
as
I
have
been
mowed
down
bought
an
aquarium
and
two
birds
the
neighbor
and
the
neighbor
and
the
neighbor
are
also
Greenlanders
I
am
ashamed
of
myself
in
the

face
of
my
children
so
the
pictures
were
set
up
and
are
now
standing
in
the
shelf
in
frames
the
last
picture
I
have
of
my
mother
is
in
me
her
head
like
a

bowling
ball
my
wife's
cold
hands
around
my
warm
dick
the
way
she
rubbed
it
is
not
an
illness
it
is
just
a
longing
for
being
unborn
are
we
the
crown
of
creation
are

we
stupid
monkeys
oranges
make
me
happy
soon
we
will
be
at
war
with
Greenlanders
because
they
are
Greenlanders
and
have
a
faith
they
are
not
to
have
a
faith
now
I
am
here

in
the
apartment
block
now
I
am
writing
I
am
reading
beams
a
load
of
fat
from
the
blubber
of
small
ball-
shaped
cakes
fat
from
being
me
without
us
nuuk
take
me
home

now
the
birds
died
on
the
balconey
but
the
fish
are
alive
I
go
down
and
sit
on
the
bench
tired
of
myself
like
a
Greendlander
throw
up
blood
like
a
Greenlander
write
make

it
look
easy
like
a
Greenlander
but
everything
is
so
hard
like
a Greenlander
shitting
ice
this
is
a
prayer
you
can
find
me
behind
all
the
medicine
we
had
been
to
a
concert
at

the
harbour
you
had
some
gin
I
squirted
you
in
the
face
in
the
evening
you
said
it
was
definitely
like
that
well,
then
all
the
other
memories
this
is
a
chain
of
lights

new
birds
mother
gave
out
from
her
home
up
to
her
death
that
is
the
memory
things
are
not
miss
you
guys
terribly
your
cunt
I
remember
as
cries
of
seagulls
a
newly
ploughed

but
it
is
the
ear
that
is
you
the
way
it
curls
on
the
left
side
we
lived
there
in
the
house
by
the
sea
all
those
years
I
take
the
blame
I
am

ready
for
a
sect
but
don't
tell
anyone
don't
reveal
that
I
am
open
warm
and
soft
and
full
of
love.

*

I'm telling you, it's cozy now
they have been decorating for Christmas
spruces hang over the dining room
and there are calendar candles
but each day is still
like opening the same lid
when I close my eyes
then I see you and your husband like Jews
and the house is surrounded by
Nazis
that's how I see it
anyway, I had a talk with my doctor yesterday
and he did not think
I should go home for Christmas
he wanted to see me through to the new year
I pray a lot to Jesus
and imagine that he can shine a light from above
so that he can look down
do you also cheat on your new husband
and hang out at the pubs in the morning
I wish you all the best in the new year
and would like to prepare you both for
a massive amount of fireworks across your thatched roof.

You can't jump out
there are no curtains
to hang yourself in
so I smash a bottle and cut my wrist.

Trouble
I get a band-aid
and may end up in the straitjacket.

it doesn't look too good for me
but we'll change to Seroquel

and see what happens
someone has clogged
all the toilets
because tiny bacteria men keep coming out of them

yesterday Glenn asked if he could
blow me

we will soon be going to the fitness room and will
feel better after the bath

there are thirteen hours until I can ask for my sleeping pill
and the band aid is keeping
me together.

We don't dance around the Christmas tree
but sing Merry Christmas
and eat duck

afterward rice pudding and Ulla takes
the almond prize
there is spruce on the ceiling
and Chritmas balls in the windows

afterward we play a present game
and I win a bottle opener
in a life buoy
and a box of matches

there is candy in the bowls and to be frank
I can't see the big difference between spending
Christmas at home
and here

except for when Glenn gets his
nose broken by the new guy
and Frandsen slides in the blood and breaks his wrist

then we sing a few psalms together again
I have diarrhea
and heartburn

but then everything picks up speed with
"In the Loft Sits the Pixy With His Christmas Porridge."

The ward is a spaceship
we've been shot
out
Glen says who got it from Bjørn

and I put out my smoke
and light a new one
we are floating in a cigar holder outside of time
and space

I drink some coffee
yesterday we got meatballs with red cabbage
and a cold buttermilk dish

you shouldn't serve a cold buttermilk dish
in the middle of winter
I say

Bjørn believes additionally that the black holes
are the holes of our minds
that for each time we dive
a new hole is created
sort of like the cavities in your teeth

our thoughts are a form of tooth decay

during the winter you should get porridge
and in the summer a cold buttermilk dish
hot cold
cold hot

but in reality it's all a film
we are mere pictures, shadows
says Glen
Bjørn says

I am Jesus
says Glen

The blood test lady passes by with her cart
one of the neon lights in the ceiling
is blinking

all power has been given to me
in heaven and on earth

his eyes have a completely empty look
and I believe him

there could be a whole universe
in that glance

I make the sign of the cross and go out to the smoker's den
the new plastic plant
has arrived

the hedge surrounding it
keeps the thoughts in place

and the rest disappears in the smoke in a square
of metered light.

This morning I get
up as a head physician
and the head physician lies back in his bed

give him a shot if he's good
I say to the nurse
as I shave

then I do the rounds
where all the other physicians
and nurses lie and
pee in their mouths

and burn the whole place down
room after room

leave the hospital the flames of which
are impingements against the winter sky
at home I sit down to some red wine
that makes me
someone else
us

I am doing better, they say.

Black bird on a roof ridge
in snowy weather

oil stain in the asphalt
sends rainbow trouts out
on the grass

cat sails in under a bush.

Lonni has organized it
there is coffee and
cookies
they come from AA with
a blue book each under their arm

they have the key
Lonni says and leaves us alone

but I'm not really in the mood
I cannot write
this poem
mountains can move faith

the AA's are all right, they are safe cattle in the herd
but I'm a wolf now
I've been there
I don't have the energy for it

you must stand on your own or fall
I say

say sorry and let the creator
remove your illness
surrender your life to God

I have prayed and prayed and prayed
and landed here
But Jesus is all right
he just doesn't have the time

you must open your heart to God
follow our program
or die

then I choose to die

as the two men leave
at the door one of them says to Lonni
that I am not at
susceptible
that those that are intellectual are the hardest.

Don't look me up
I don't want to recieve visits when you come out
forget the money
they are a present
don't call, either
best, Søren.

Today I'm going to a meeting
about going back home
I know you are nervous and have gotten
an extra lock on the door
it's wonderful that the kids have removed all the bottles
I'll be driving with Falck
and already have a plan
I'm going to write a novel and get
more out and meet people
I'm not to sit there and snuggle up
says the doctor
Of course, I cannot drink
but I can water the flowers and go down to the laundry room
that is how ordinary I've become
now
I hope you had a good Christmas
here we got both duck and marzipan
we weren't in want of anything
the new medicine helps me to stay composed
I have gotten a sponsor in AA
I just need to believe in God
anyway
I won't bore you with all of that
I just wanted to say that I am
doing well and that you won't be needing that extra lock
I would be able to smash
a window if I had to
or go through the basement.

Poul refuses to take a shit
in his toilet, a cleaning company
has to come
he says

I stay neutral between Lonni and him
but agree with Lonni
that he cannot continue shitting on the floor

other than that there's not much to tell
I won't be moving to
the open ward
I'll be coming directly home with the regional psychiatric center
following right behind me

and a big box of pills

yesterday one of the dangerous ones walked up close to me
and whispered:
I always had this desire to kill

Ulla and Glenn had anal sex in the cleaning room
so her intestine is bleeding
Glenn has been moved

one of the nurses just had a grandchild
Lonni has two
you can't help but loving
the little darlings

*

My sister
and I are driven home in each our own car

the streets are filled with wet gunpowder
most of the houses
have their curtains drawn

see you, we say
see you.

MIKAEL JOSEPHSEN has a special eye for the nature of addiction and writes especially well about society's forgotten and the mentally ill. He has received a Danish Fiction Writers Honorary Award. Most recently, Josephsen has completed his autobiographical abuse trilogy, the poetry collections *Break, I Am Grandma,* and *An Idiot's Jubilation.*

www.ingramcontent.com/pod-product-compliance
Lightning Source LLC
Chambersburg PA
CBHW011217120626
46545CB00008B/3027

* 9 7 8 1 9 5 6 0 0 5 8 9 9 *